A little more than a moment

Sabrina Szola

BookLeaf Publishing

India | USA | UK

Presentation by *BookLeaf Publishing*

Web: www.bookleafpub.com

E-mail: info@bookleafpub.com

ISBN: 978-93-5744-999-1

First edition 2022

Inside your head

The crisp leaves blanketing the ground
The cool air wrapping around your lungs
The darkness settling on the horizon
Nothing but silence surrounding you
Heart pounding in your ears
Breathing on your neck
You take off, running
The sound bouncing in your head
The feeling of claws grasping for your legs
Fear consuming you as you dash inside
Panting, you lock up
From the demons inside your head

Creature under the bed

Tucked in so tight
Blanket to my chin
Growling from under the bed
Claws curling up from below
Holding my breath
It's eyes piercing from the darkness
The teeth glistening in a sickly smile
Voice caught in my throat
Swallow back my scream
As it starts to devour me
Piece by piece

Why the room spins

Heart beating
Room spinning
Everything blurs
You standing alone
Breath caught in my chest
Knees weak
Shaking hands
I forgot my words
Home, the word
Screaming through my head
Never feeling alone
This is where I'm meant to be

Less of yourself

When the day rolls around
The clouds seep in
Around you the smoke rises
The sounds slip in the distance
The light focuses on it
It's grip tightens the waves of feelings
It's controls you, overwhelming
As I choke it back
I watch as I become less of myself

Missing someone

In a blink of the eye it becomes like a monster. Heart races or skips a beat, nervous and shaky. As you doze off that sound awakes you. Always wondering if you are good enough, will you miss that chance, that notification. Day after day less sleep replaced with ache. Maybe one day you'll be redeemed, have another chance. That's the life of missing someone

Take the flow

They're nothing like opioids
which balance the human body
on a knife's blade edge
between pleasure and death.
The sting of the movement
Thin lines showing we're real
Numb, dumb and broken
Watching through the filter
Shattered like mirrors
Reflections of who we are
You will always have my heart
Even when I lose my mind

Do you wonder?

Do you ever look up at the stars and wonder if I'm staring also? If we are sharing the same moment, staring at the moon and just enjoying the night sky. Do you miss the things that were ours? Even a little. Do you crave the sound of my voice the same way I crave yours? If I could call you straight out would you panic to try and answer. Knowing that come morning we were each others first thought, first message, before we even crawled out of bed. Do you stay up at night missing me, considering to reach out? Or is this just me hoping? Wondering if one day I'll be your world as much as your mine.

To live another day

Breathing shouldn't be so hard
Like swallowing salt water
Each breath in
I'm drowning, suffocating
In a room full of people
You watch me choking
Watch me beg for release
Beg for you to let me breathe
The water drains from around me
No longer floating, lingering
To live another day

Hand

I hold out my hand
The breeze passes over
Awaiting your warmth
Moments that we talk
Let us watch the sun come up
Skipping rocks hand in hand
You held me tight
Crossing the street
Firm and comforting
I held tight as you took your last breath
Now I hold out my hand
Wishing it didn't have to end

You'll never understand

From the moment the sun rises
Til the the moon comes out
My world revolves around you
The way your smile curls ever so little
Your eyes light up with bewilderment
At the slightest excitement
The feel you give off just being you
The laugh that escapes your lips
In pure enjoyment at the tiny things
The quirky hand motions
The words that play in my head
in your voice, they live rent free
Something about you
So mesmerizing, captivating
Makes my heart race
Every scar a story for someone to discover
Every story a moment for someone to earn
These are just some of the reasons
You'll never understand
What I see in you

For two minutes

Sometimes we forget
The simplest actions
How they effect us
Making your bed
Being surrounded by you
By your scent
It's never been so sweet
So natural, so arousing
Simple yet fulfilling
For two minutes
I feel like I'm where
I'm meant to be
For two minutes
I know how to be yours

Angel of Death

Ocean blue eyes
Smoke slipping from between
Ruby red lips
Locks of hair
Fall into her face
That smile
Quick flash
I'm taken aback
Breathless, It's sudden
Heart stops
Eyes bulge
Her lips press against mine
She claims me
Angel of Death

Close my eyes to sleep

As I close my eyes to sleep
Let me dance in the moon
Play among the stars
Clouds that lead me home

As I close my eyes to sleep
Watch me count some sheep
One by one
Taking the leap

As I close my eyes to sleep
Sounds fade away
Light is swallowed up
I float away
As I close my eyes to sleep

Are you scared?

The sting of the words
The burn of the drink
Takes hold, choking me
Hurting, gut wretched
Drowning in tears
Anger swelling to break
It takes the wheel
Driving straight into a wall
Fist makes connections
The sound of gunshots
Friction of the movement
You bite at my throat
Wishing to draw blood
I pull you in tight
Wishing to taste the fear
Are you scared?
Are you mine?
It pools around you
The darkness eating you alive
The life leaving your eyes
With your nails digging out flesh
The next glass so much smoother
The smell of pain
As I gasp

The smile

The way we look at things
Simple as a smile
Cheek to cheek
The dimple marks on some
The blank slate on others
Whether your teeth flash
Or they remain hidden
We hold so much emotion
All in a simple action
Contagious like a virus
They can change the world
Your smile onto me
My smile takes fire

Home

The place we're meant to be
The place we end up
Aren't always the same
But as long as I'm with you
I'll call it home

Until the stars stop shining
And the sun doesn't come up
As long as I'm with you
I'll call it home

Whether we shine bright
Or need to sit in the dark
As long as I'm with you
It will be my home

Perfect flaws

Nobody is perfect
Not society's perfect
But everything about you
Screams mine
My perfection
Every flaw you may have
The scars you try and hide
The ones you can't
The history in your eyes
Perfection
See where you came from
What you have survived
If I could ever measure up
These are your unique things
Quirks, and ways to cope
For everything I see
Is one more reason
To know who you are
To love you
Your perfect flaws

Your song

The sound of your voice
I'm lost in the song
Sweet and gentle melody
The world around us fades
The topic doesn't matter
It's all you and all us
I could listen all day
Never tire of the lull
Music that lives within me
Forever and always

Hauntingly Beautiful

The moment I close my eyes
I see you standing there
I feel your breath on my ear
I hear you whisper my name
The seduction of your lullaby
Your teeth against my willing throat
My heart beating like a drum
I feel the blood streaming down
Rivets falling on my chest
My eyes open to your pale eyes
Your scent so sweet
So calming, so soothing
Finish me like the best meal
You've ever had

The bad guys

Where he touches your skin
The scorches appear
Devil sweetly whispers in your ear
Wolf in sheep's clothing
Leading you to slaughter
Lulling you like a siren
With his broken promises
And honeyed words
Dangling the bait
Red flags like roses
By the dozen, counting
Draining you, mind scramble
Trapped in barb wire
He claws you tightly
In his clutch
As you start to walk through flames
Like lava
You always liked the bad guys

What if I told you

What if I told you
Everytime I look in your eyes
I see a thousand lives I'll never have

What if i told you
Everytime I hear your voice
I hear the words I can only dream of

What if I told you
Everytime I'm by you
I crave the touch I'll never earn

What if I told you
I love you so bad it aches
Would you look at me the same?